History in Evidence

SAXON BRITAIN

Tony D. Triggs

History in Evidence

Medieval Britain

Norman Britain

Prehistoric Britain

Roman Britain

Saxon Britain

Tudor Britain

Victorian Britain

Viking Britain

300 419343

Cover design: Alison Anholt-White
Series design: Helen White
Consultant: Dr Margaret L Faull

Cover pictures: The main picture is St Lawrence
Church, Bradford on Avon. The inset is a gold buckle
from the Sutton Hoo excavations in Suffolk.

First published in 1989 by
Wayland (Publishers) Limited
61 Western Road, Hove
East Sussex BN3 1JD, England

British Library Cataloguing in Publication Data
Triggs, Tony D.
  Saxon Britain.
  1. Anglo-Saxon civilisation. Archaeological sources
  I. Title II. Series
  942.01

HARDBACK ISBN 1–85210–575–5

PAPERBACK ISBN 0–7502–0542–3

Edited and typeset by Kudos, Hove, East Sussex
Printed in Italy by G. Canale & C.S.p.A., Turin
Bound in France by A.G.M.

Picture acknowledgements
The publishers wish to thank the following for permis-
sion to reproduce their illustrations on the pages
mentioned: Michael Holford *cover* (both), 11 (right), 26,
27, 28 (left); Cliff Lines 6; The Mansell Collection 13, 14;
C. M. Dixon/Photoresources 17 (right); Sheffield City
Museums 29; Ronald Sheridan/The Ancient Art &
Architecture Collection 17 (left), 19, 20, 21 (both), 23,
28 (right); Tony D. Triggs 7. The remaining pictures are
from the Wayland Picture Library. The artwork was
supplied by the following: Mark Bergin 22-3; Malcolm
S. Walker 4, 5, 7, 8, 9, 10, 12, 15, 19; Stephen Wheele
16, 25, 26, 29.

Contents

Who were the Saxons?.......5

Finding Saxon sites............6

A Saxon village..................8

The potter.......................10

Food and drink..................12

Spinning and weaving.......14

Clothes and jewellery........16

Fun and games..................18

Religion............................20

Monastery life..................23

A royal burial....................24

The lives of the poor.........27

Weapons and war..............28

Places to visit....................30

Glossary...........................31

Books to read....................31

Index................................32

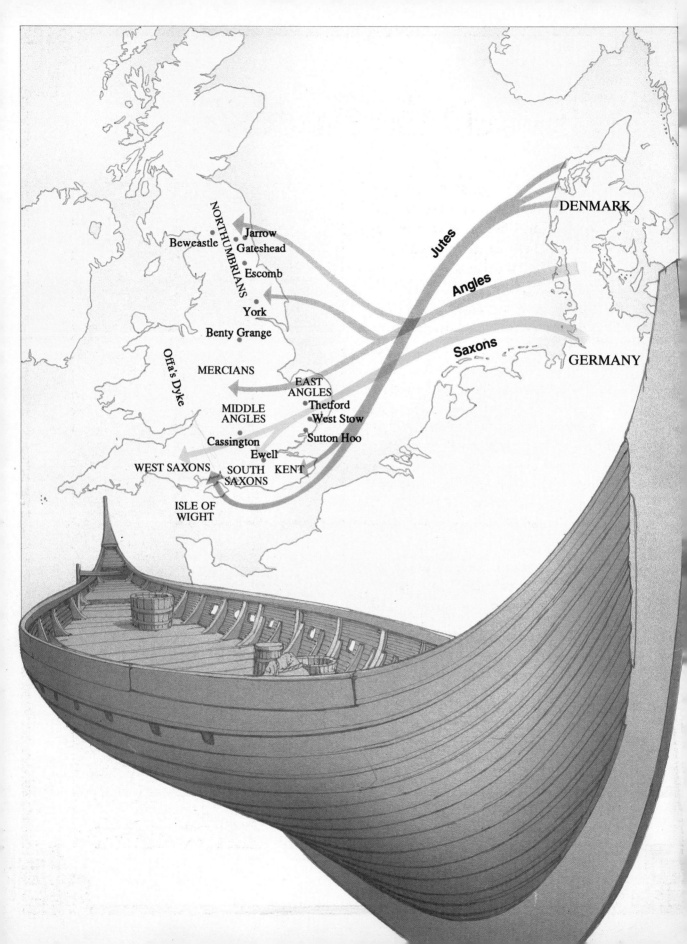

DENMARK

Jutes

Angles

Saxons

GERMANY

NORTHUMBRIANS

Jarrow
Bewcastle
Gateshead

Escomb

York

Benty Grange

Offa's Dyke

MERCIANS

EAST
ANGLES

Thetford
West Stow

MIDDLE
ANGLES

Sutton Hoo

Cassington
Ewell

WEST SAXONS   SOUTH   KENT
SAXONS

ISLE OF
WIGHT

Who were the Saxons?

In the fifth century AD, large groups of tribes from northern Europe rowed across the stormy North Sea in search of new land. Most of them settled in England and Scotland, and their descendants still live in Britain today.

There are various clues that tell us where these people came from. Among the most important clues are ancient documents. In the eighth century a Saxon monk, called Bede, lived and worked in a monastery at Jarrow, in northern England. Bede wrote a book called *A History of the English Church and People*, and in it he said that the settlers had come from the three most fearsome races of Germany: the Saxons, Angles and Jutes. We usually group all the settlers together and call them the Saxons.

Place names still remind us of the different groups of Saxon settlers. For example, Essex means 'East Saxons' land', Sussex means 'South Saxons' land' and East Anglia means 'the eastern part of the Angles' land'.

OPPOSITE This map shows where the Saxons came from in northern Europe and the areas of Britain in which they settled. They rowed across the North Sea in long, wooden boats, like the one shown, which carried up to 50 men. All the places mentioned in this book are also shown on the map.

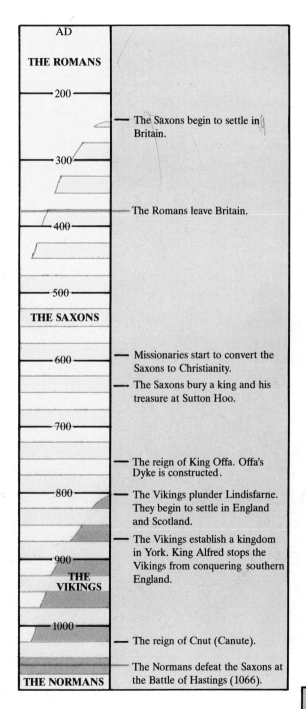

AD

THE ROMANS

— 200 —

The Saxons begin to settle in Britain.

— 300 —

The Romans leave Britain.

— 400 —

— 500 —

THE SAXONS

— 600 —

Missionaries start to convert the Saxons to Christianity.

The Saxons bury a king and his treasure at Sutton Hoo.

— 700 —

The reign of King Offa. Offa's Dyke is constructed.

— 800 —

The Vikings plunder Lindisfarne. They begin to settle in England and Scotland.

The Vikings establish a kingdom in York. King Alfred stops the Vikings from conquering southern England.

— 900 —

THE VIKINGS

— 1000 —

The reign of Cnut (Canute).

The Normans defeat the Saxons at the Battle of Hastings (1066).

THE NORMANS

Finding Saxon sites

The Saxons settled in villages, which they built of wood. Each Saxon village consisted of a group of huts; these were the Saxons' homes, workshops, barns and sheds. In addition, the Saxons usually built a wooden hall or meeting-house. A village might contain only a single family, but this would include all the uncles, aunts and other relatives. The Saxons lived by farming; if their crops had failed, they would probably have starved.

Because they were built of wood, most Saxon buildings have disappeared. However, many towns and villages in England and southern Scotland have grown up on sites which the Saxons chose, and most of them have Saxon names.

A few of the places where the Saxons built their villages were never used again. Their remains have often been ploughed

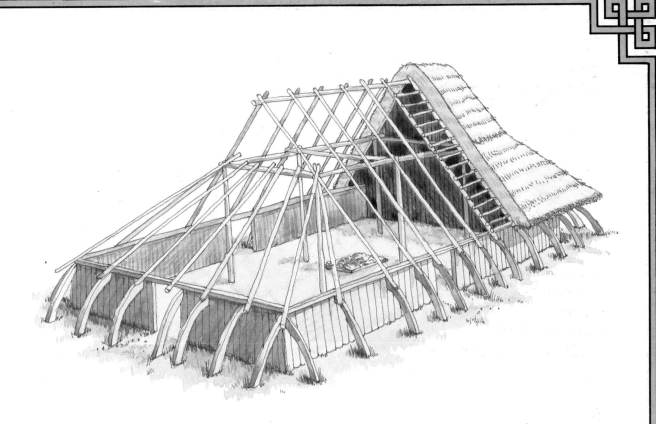

ABOVE A large hall, like this one, would have housed a Saxon king and his servants.

up and destroyed. Fragments of pottery lying in a field today may mark the place where Saxon children worked and played over a thousand years ago.

Photographs taken from the air can be helpful: they sometimes show where buried remains are affecting crops, and if they are taken when the sun is low in the sky, they may show ridges or hollows made by farmers or builders long ago.

OPPOSITE A view of some of the reconstructed houses at West Stow, in Suffolk. West Stow gives us an idea of what a typical Saxon village looked like.

ABOVE All the Saxon buildings in a village were made of wood. Here, a hall is being built to test ideas about the construction methods used by the Saxons.

A Saxon village

Archaeologists have discovered that some homes had floors built over the pits inside them.

In the fifth century some Saxon settlers built a village at West Stow in Suffolk, but they moved away 200 years later. The houses quickly fell into ruins and disappeared. The site was forgotten for centuries, but in the 1940s someone found pieces of pottery there. Archaeologists dug up the grass and weeds and they noticed patterns of dark-coloured spots in the sand underneath. They realized that the Saxons' houses had been built with a framework of wooden posts (like the metal girders used today). The posts had stood in the sand, and the spots showed where they had rotted away.

Other clues showed that most buildings had had a flat-bottomed pit inside them. This was puzzling. Did the Saxons live and work in these pits or did they put floors over them? Eventually, the archaeologists found some clues. In one of the pits they came across the skeleton of a dog. The skull was separate and it had rolled away from the rest of the bones. This suggested that the dog had died, then rotted and fallen apart undisturbed. This could only have happened *under* a floor. (The Saxons must have put up with the horrible smell for months.)

In another hut the archaeologists found a hearth on which the Saxons had burned some logs to keep warm. The hearth was made of clay and it must have been meant to protect the floor-boards from being burnt. However, the building where the hearth was found had been burnt down. This helped the archaeologists, since charred things sometimes survive in the soil instead of rotting away. They found the remains of planks from the walls and the floor of the building. They also found twigs from the thatched roof.

The archaeologists tried rebuilding some of the Saxon huts and they found that rain could not get in through the thatch, but smoke could get out.

There is still a question which archaeologists have to answer, that is: why did the Saxons dig pits in their huts, then cover them?

Saxon buildings had an uncovered, flat-bottomed pit for their floor.

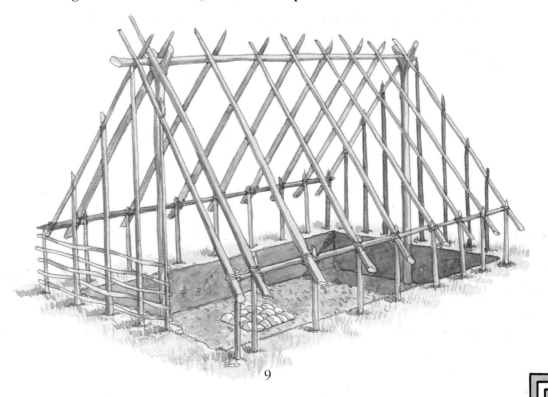

The potter

Pots were made in many Saxon villages. Clay was dug up and often sand and horse dung was added to it to make the pots stronger. Sometimes villagers pushed the clay into shape with their fingers. At other times they rolled it into very long 'snakes', then coiled them up to make the pot.

At a place called Cassington, in Oxfordshire, archaeologists have found the remains of the special oven (called a kiln) where the Saxon villagers baked their pots. The first thing the archaeologists found was a reddened patch in the stony soil. It was round and it measured a metre across. The redness had been caused by heat, and the archaeologists found ashes and pieces of scorched pottery. They also found the base of a little wall that went all

> Only a few Saxon kilns have survived, but place names, like Pottersbury and Potterton, show where others once stood.

Temporary dome of wicker and clay (destroyed)

Firing floor

Stoke hole

Pottery

A kiln would have looked like the one shown here. The dome would have been destroyed each time the potter baked some pots.

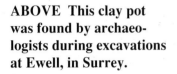

ABOVE This clay pot was found by archaeologists during excavations at Ewell, in Surrey.

RIGHT A large jug, with two handles and a spout, which was unearthed at Thetford, in Norfolk. It was found in pieces and carefully put together to display in a museum. It was used for ale or mead.

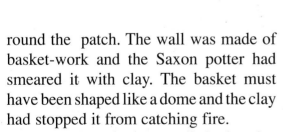

round the patch. The wall was made of basket-work and the Saxon potter had smeared it with clay. The basket must have been shaped like a dome and the clay had stopped it from catching fire.

At one place there was a dip in the edge of the reddened area. This led down to a shallow pit where the Saxons had burned a bonfire. Hot air from the bonfire had entered the kiln and gone out through a hole in the top. The flow of air made the pots really hot and it baked them hard. When the pots were ready, the potter had to put out the fire, destroy the kiln, and remove the pots. If he wanted to bake a new batch of pots, he had to build another dome. This involved a lot of work; archaeologists sometimes find the bottoms of several domes when they study a kiln.

The Saxons also made things out of metal. To do this they used furnaces which were rather like kilns.

Food and drink

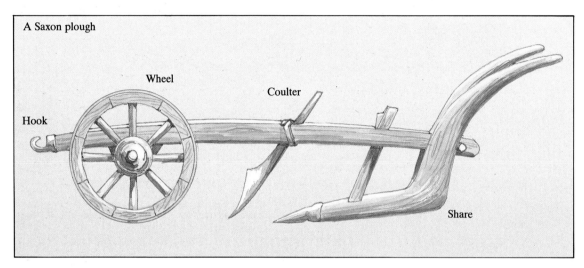

A Saxon plough

Wheel

Coulter

Hook

Share

This is what a farmer would have used to plough his fields. It would have been pulled by oxen.

What did the Saxons eat and drink? Place names often give us clues about their diet. For example, Appleton means 'apple farm' or 'apple village'.

Clues in the soil can help us too, for seeds and husks can survive for many hundreds of years. At West Stow, archaeologists have found the remains of wheat, barley, rye and various other crops in some of the huts. Two lots of barley seemed to be charred. In one case the Saxons' granary had probably been destroyed in a blaze. In the other case, the Saxons probably burned the crop because it contained some poisonous seeds. Losing their crop must have meant that theSaxons went hungry for several months.

We can find out more about the Saxons'

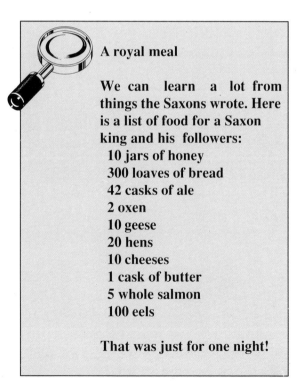

A royal meal

We can learn a lot from things the Saxons wrote. Here is a list of food for a Saxon king and his followers:
10 jars of honey
300 loaves of bread
42 casks of ale
2 oxen
10 geese
20 hens
10 cheeses
1 cask of butter
5 whole salmon
100 eels

That was just for one night!

food by studying their pottery. Villagers often made their own pots, and they sometimes got seeds in the clay by mistake. When a pot was baked, the seeds burned away, leaving tiny pits, which show what sort of seed was there. Barley grains often got mixed with the clay, and this suggests that one person must have been shaping a pot in the family hut while someone else was using barley to make a stew or a tub of ale.

Nowadays, nosy newspaper reporters sometimes raid people's dustbins to find out about their diet and their way of life. Archaeologists like to find out about the Saxons in a similar way – by examining their rubbish dumps. Bones are among the commonest finds. They show that the Saxons ate sheep, cattle, pigs, goats, deer, swans, poultry and all sorts of other birds.

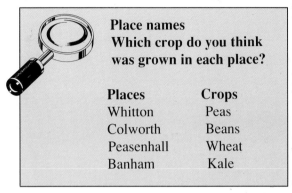

Place names
Which crop do you think was grown in each place?

Places	Crops
Whitton	Peas
Colworth	Beans
Peasenhall	Wheat
Banham	Kale

ABOVE This painting from a Saxon book shows three noblemen enjoying a feast. They are being served food by two of their slaves.

Spinning and weaving

The Saxons turned sheep's wool into cloth. We know this because archaeologists sometimes find shears, combs and other items used for this type of work. The Saxons used shears to get the wool from their sheep; then they combed out all the tangles and dirt.

Next the wool was spun into thread. Women usually did this job. They needed a stick (called a spindle) fitted with a circular weight (called a spindle whorl). The woman attached the wool to her spindle and started it spinning. The weight kept it going, and it drew more wool between her fingers, twisting it into a really strong thread, called the yarn. The wooden spindles have rotted away since Saxon times, but the whorls, which were usually made of clay, are often discovered on Saxon sites.

The women wove their yarn into cloth on upright looms. They began by tying threads of yarn to the crossbar at the top of the loom.   They wanted these hanging

In this drawing from a Saxon book, a woman is using a loom like the one on the next page.

threads to be as taut as possible, so they weighted them with rings made of clay. The women wove more woollen yarn from side to side, going over and under the hanging threads. They pushed the new strands of yarn together with 'beating swords', and these are sometimes found in the ground. Archaeologists also find lots of loom-weights. They look like doughnuts and sometimes they are found in rows. This suggests that a hut and a loom were destroyed by fire. As the threads burned away, the weights fell neatly on to the ground.

The Saxon women made the villagers' clothes from the cloth. If they had any spare cloth, they tried selling it in nearby villages. Some Saxon cloth was exported to Europe. We know this because of an angry letter which one of the Saxons' European customers wrote. He said they were sending shorter cloaks than he had ordered. Perhaps the Saxons were trying to cheat!

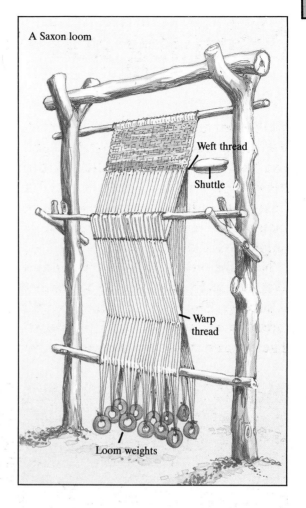

A Saxon loom

Weft thread

Shuttle

Warp thread

Loom weights

Loom weights found by archaeologists.

Clothes and jewellery

Woollen cloak. The man's other clothes were probably made of wool or skins.

Clothes made of linen for comfort.

Shoes made of leather.

A nobleman and his wife in their fine clothes.

ABOVE LEFT A piece of jewellery found at Sutton Hoo. It belonged to King Redwald.

ABOVE RIGHT This brooch was once worn by a rich woman in Kent.

As well as making woollen cloth, the Saxons made cloth from the stems of nettles. They beat the stems and dried the fibres, then spun and wove them. This type of cloth must have given the Saxons very itchy skin.

Towns grew up in Saxon Britain, and the wealthier townsfolk could buy themselves comfortable linen cloth. Like other cloth, the Saxons coloured it with dyes from plants, and the women sometimes embroidered it too.

We can see Saxon garments in pictures they drew. Garments rarely survive in the soil, but in Denmark there are bogs where the water preserves dead bodies and even clothes. Certain bodies found in these bogs have been there since the time when the Saxons came to Britain, so they show us what the Saxons would have worn.

Cutting rough cloth into interesting shapes would have made it fray, so most Saxons wrapped themselves up in cloaks.

Next to the skin the women wore gowns, while the Saxon men wore simple tunics and trousers.

Unlike clothing, jewellery is often found. This is because it was made of metal and precious stones, which rarely dissolve away in the ground. Village girls wore cross-shaped brooches made of bronze. Sometimes exactly the same brooches have been found in different places, which suggests that they were made by the same person and sold by a pedlar on his travels. The Saxons had slaves, who could not afford any jewellery at all.

Rich people wore very fine jewellery. This was made out of silver or gold and was sometimes studded with precious stones. Saxon kings had the finest jewellery of all. One king had beautiful golden clasps to fasten his cloak at the shoulders. The separate halves of the clasp were sewn to the cloak and the king did them up with golden pins.

Fun and games

The Saxons worked hard but they also knew how to enjoy themselves. Music was one of their greatest pleasures, and fragments of Saxon lyres (very small harps) have been found. Experts have rebuilt one of the lyres, and it gives an idea of the soft, mysterious, twanging tone of Saxon music.

Lyres were used to accompany singing or poetry at Saxon feasts. The Saxons liked feasting and always had plenty of ale and mead. They passed a lyre round and they sang or recited verse in turn. The words told of heroes from long ago in the Saxons' past. Sometimes the stories were true and sometimes they were too good to be true! True or not, they were nearly always very exciting. One of the Saxons' favourite stories was a long poem about Beowulf. Beowulf was a Swedish prince who killed two monsters and died when he tried to kill a third. We can still read the poem; it takes several hours, and the Saxons must have trembled with excitement as they listened in their hall at night round their crackling fires.

The Saxons liked riddles as well as tales of adventure. See if you can work out

A Saxon riddle (answer on page 30)
An enemy robbed me of life. He removed my skin, soaked it in water, then took it and spread it out in the sun. The sun and my enemy's knife caused it to lose its hair and its roughness. Next it was folded up. A feather moved over its surface and left wise markings behind. It swallowed more dye and again made its mark. Lastly, a man put covers upon it. What was it?

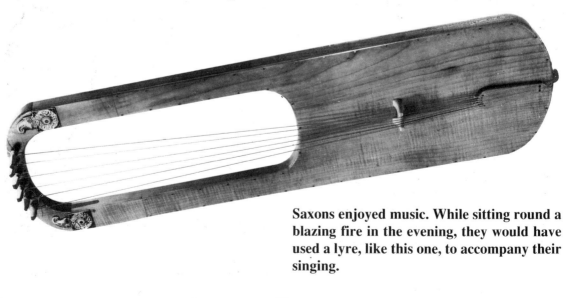

Saxons enjoyed music. While sitting round a blazing fire in the evening, they would have used a lyre, like this one, to accompany their singing.

18

A *tæfl* board

The Saxons played a board-game called *tæfl* (see the diagram). Black and white move one piece per turn either forwards, backwards or sideways. A piece can be moved any number of squares, but it has to stop if another piece is in its way. A piece is taken if the other side gets it sandwiched.

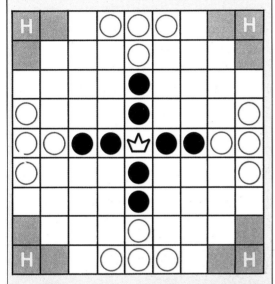

○ Starting squares for white.
● Starting squares for black.
♔ The king's square.

▨ Squares which white must not go on to.
H Home squares for the king.

White takes black

Black wins the game if he gets the king home to one of the corners. White wins if he gets black surrounded, takes the king or blocks its way to all the corners. Make yourself a *tæfl* board, make or find some suitable pieces and try out the game.

the riddle opposite. The Saxons also loved to play board games. We know this because archaeologists have found all sorts of counters and playing pieces.

The Saxons liked outdoor activities too. They wrote about horse-racing and today there are places with names like Plaistow, which means 'playing-field', where the Saxons once played sports. Children probably made themselves leather footballs, which they stuffed full of feathers or unwanted wool.

Saxon women probably enjoyed doing embroidery and needlework. We know this because many Saxons liked to be buried with their favourite possessions, and beautiful work-boxes are often found in women's graves.

ABOVE An ivory knight for a chess board.

Religion

A gold ring with runes (magical letters) written on it to stop wounds bleeding.

When the Saxons came to Britain, they were pagans. They believed in many gods and they tried to please them by sacrificing people and animals. Some of the people found in bogs in Denmark had nooses round their necks, and their stomachs contained a special porridge made of seeds. The Saxons may have made them eat it, then put them to death as a way of asking the gods for good harvests.

Place names also give us clues about the Saxons' religion. Gateshead means 'goat's head'; the local Saxons probably worshipped goats' heads which they put on stakes in forest clearings. The Saxons called November 'Bloodmonth', so perhaps this was the time of the year when they sacrificed animals.

The Saxons used spells and lucky charms. A ring has been found with a spell written in ancient letters, known as runes. The spell was supposed to stop wounds from bleeding.

In the seventh century, missionaries encouraged the Saxons to become Christians. According to Bede, the monk and scholar, an East Anglian king called Redwald was not sure what to believe, so he put a Christian altar beside the pagan one in his temple.

As the Saxons became Christians, they built many churches. They also put up crosses to mark the places where they worshipped in the open air. Monasteries were built, and the monks copied out the Christian Gospels in beautiful lettering. These Gospels are among the finest treasures surviving from Saxon times.

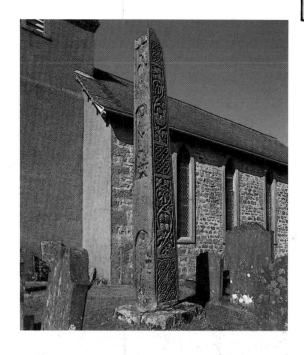

ABOVE The Saxon cross at Bewcastle.

This church, built around AD 800, can be seen at Escomb, in County Durham.

The monastery at Jarrow in the days of the scholar Bede.

Monastery life

In Saxon Britain, the only children who went to school were the ones whose parents sent them to live in monasteries. They worked and prayed with the monks, and they studied in the monastery school-room. When they grew up they, too, became monks.

Life in a monastery was very hard. The pupils and monks slept in dormitories, and every day they had to get up for prayers at two o'clock in the morning. After that, there were prayers every two or three hours until evening.

Monasteries produced nearly all their own food and other requirements. Most monks had to work in the gardens, fields and workshops belonging to the monastery. A few monks spent nearly all their time making beautiful books, and the other monks had to keep them supplied with animal skins to use as paper.

The monks drew pictures that show them at work, and archaeologists have dug up some of their tools, including pointed ones for marking designs on the skins. Pupils had to practise on tablets of beeswax. When there was no more room on their tablets, they smoothed the surface and started again.

The monastery at Jarrow was built of stone, and the foundations have survived in the ground. As well as church buildings and workshops, there was a kitchen, a dining-room, a dormitory and a hostel for travellers. Deciding how buildings were used can be difficult, but we know where the dining-room stood because bones and shells from fish have been found in the ground. In this area, there was also the base of a reading stand: the monks and pupils had to eat in silence while someone read to them from the Bible.

The monks obtained their water and fish from the nearby river. (Archaeologists have discovered the monks' fishing tackle.) The workshops were built near the water's edge, and clues in the soil show that some were used for metalwork and others for making colourful stained-glass windows.

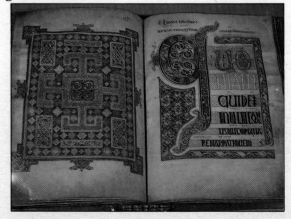

ABOVE Some monks produced books in their monasteries. Often, they would spend hours decorating the pages with coloured ink. These designs were drawn by monks on Lindisfarne.

A royal burial

The Saxons believed in a life after death, and they put people's possessions in their graves so that they could go on using them. As a result, archaeologists find all sorts of things in Saxon cemeteries.

The most famous Saxon cemetery is at Sutton Hoo in Suffolk. Each grave is marked with a grassy mound several metres across, and in 1939 archaeologists began to excavate the largest one. They soon found a pattern of stains in the soil. The grave had contained a wooden ship and the stains showed where it had rotted away. The archaeologists cleared out the soil, expecting to find a skeleton, but, to their surprise, there were no bones at all. However, they found all sorts of precious objects made of silver and gold. Some had come from the lid of a purse. The rest of the purse (made of fur and bone) had

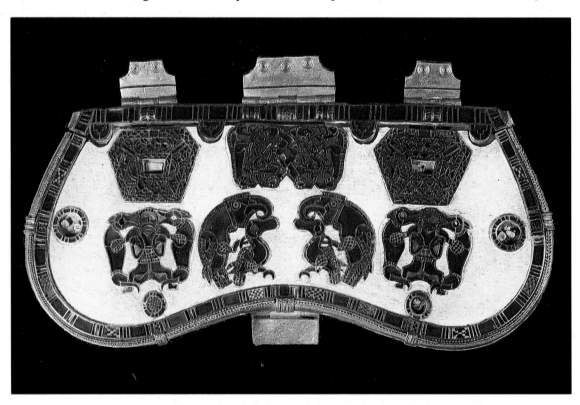

Many precious objects were found in King Redwald's grave at Sutton Hoo. Here is one of them. It is the lid of a purse, which is made out of gold and studded with jewels.

rotted away. Could a whole body have rotted away? The archaeologists carried out chemical tests on the soil, and they found that a body had once been there.

The things found in the grave were so precious and grand that they must have belonged to a king or a prince. There were jewels from a sword and a scabbard, a buckle made of solid gold, a warrior's helmet and a huge whetstone. Whetstones are rods of very rough stone used for sharpening blades. However, the whetstone at Sutton Hoo had never been used. It was so enormous it looked like a mace, and a king had probably carried it to show his importance.

1. The helmet hid the king's face, so a moustache and eyebrows were included in the design.

2. The round shield was made of wood and leather, with metal fittings.

King Redwald probably dressed like this when he went into battle. Notice the purse hanging from the belt around his waist. His helmet is shown on page 28.

3. Purse decorated with jewels (see the photograph on the opposite page). This reminded the king's followers that they would get a rich reward if they served him well.

The purse had contained about 40 gold coins and these gave a clue to the king's identity. They had all been made in about 620, so the king must have died soon after that. According to Bede, the East Anglian kings had a palace at Rendlesham, very near to the cemetery. Bede also says that Redwald died in 624, so the Sutton Hoo grave probably belonged to him.

Saxons often had to clear trees away
before they could farm the land.
This man is going to use his pickaxe to
remove some roots from the soil.

Imitation keys to
show she is not a
slave.

Knife

Unlike the noble woman on page 16,
this poorer woman has to put up
with rough woollen clothing.

The lives of the poor

The graves of poor Saxons contain things, such as tools, weapons, brooches, playing counters and drinking horns, that tell us about their daily lives, too. Saxon women were sometimes buried with girdle hangers. Girdle hangers look like keys, and women wore them to show that they had a house of their own and were not slaves.

The words 'lord' and 'lady' suggest that Saxon husbands expected their wives to obey them. 'Lord' is based on the Saxon words meaning 'keeper of the bread'; 'lady' comes from the Saxon words meaning 'maker of the bread'. In other words, the wife made the bread but the husband decided who should have it. It seems that slaves received a fair share since the Saxons sometimes called them 'loaf-eaters'.

Words are not the only clue that the Saxons had slaves. Graves are sometimes found without any possessions inside them. If the rest of the graves in a cemetery have all sorts of goods, the graves without them probably belonged to slaves.

Sometimes a slave was buried just above his master or mistress, so that he or she would still have a servant after death. In some double graves it is clear that the slave was buried alive; the skeleton shows that the person died in a crouching position, and occasionally there is a heavy stone, which must have been thrown on top of the person to hold him or her down. Some archaeologists think that stones were also placed on the bodies of evil people to stop their spirits from leaving their graves.

By studying bones, archaeologists can usually tell what sex a person was, and roughly what age they were when they died. They can sometimes tell what illness or injuries the person had suffered, too. Saxons rarely lived to be older than 40, and their teeth were often badly worn from biting on grit which had come off the millstones, used for grinding the wheat into flour, and got into their bread.

Before they became Christians, the Saxons usually burned dead people and buried their ashes in pottery urns like this one.

Weapons and war

Saxon swords, shields and helmets have all been found in the soil. The helmet in Redwald's grave was enormous – he must have put padding inside it before he put it on. It is so magnificent that some people think that it was only used for important ceremonies and not for battles.

Another helmet was found at York. Like the Sutton Hoo one, it had hinged cheek guards for the warrior's cheeks. However, one of the cheek guards seemed to be missing when the helmet was found.

The archaeologists took the helmet, still full of soil, to the local hospital. They used the hospital's X-ray machine, and this revealed two objects inside it. One was a piece of chain-mail which had protected the back of the warrior's neck. The other was the missing cheek guard. The archaeologists knew that they would have to empty the helmet carefully, since the hidden parts would be rusty and delicate. Archaeologists often use equipment, like X-ray machines, in their work.

The picture on the left shows the remains of King Redwald's helmet as they were discovered in the soil. On the right is a reconstruction of King Redwald's helmet.

ABOVE The Benty Grange helmet.

1. Good luck charm.

2. Chain-mail to give protection in battle.

3. Decorated scabbard for the sword.

In 1848 a damaged helmet was found at Benty Grange, in Derbyshire. In those days archaeologists were not very good at preserving things, and many parts of the helmet were lost. However, we can see the framework of metal bands which was used in all Saxon helmets. We can also see a wild pig on top. This was meant to bring good luck to the wearer, since the pig was connected with the god Frey.

The Saxons sometimes built defences round their towns. They dug a ditch and used the soil to make an earth wall; then they fixed a sturdy fence on top. Saxons could patrol the wall to keep enemies out.

The longest wall of all was Offa's Dyke (named after one of the Saxon kings). This did not go round a town. It was built along the borders of England and Wales, and many parts can still be seen.

This is what a Saxon warrior would have worn into battle.

Places to visit

Churches, monasteries and cemeteries
Bradford-on-Avon, Wiltshire
Bradwell-on-Sea, Essex
Brixworth, Northamptonshire
Canterbury, Kent
Conisborough, South Yorkshire
Earls Barton, Northamptonshire
Escomb, County Durham
Ledsham, West Yorkshire
Lindisfarne, Northumberland
North Elmham, Norfolk
Sutton Hoo Royal Cemetery, Suffolk

Crosses
Bewcastle, Cumbria
Ilkley, West Yorkshire
Middleton, North Yorkshire
Ruthwell, Dumfriesshire
Whitby, North Yorkshire

Earthworks
Offa's Dyke, which is best seen north of
   Knighton, Powys

Reconstructed Saxon huts
West Stow, near Bury St
   Edmunds, Suffolk

Town defences
Wallingford, Oxfordshire
Wareham, Dorset

Museums
Ashmolean Museum, Oxford
Bede Monastery Museum, Jarrow
British Museum, London
Hull City Museum, Hull
Moyses Hall Museum, Bury St
   Edmunds
Museum of London, London
National Museum of Antiquities of
   Scotland, Edinburgh
Norwich Castle Museum, Norwich
Sheffield City Museum, Sheffield
University Museum of Archaeology and
   Anthropology, Cambridge
Yorkshire Museum, York

Illuminated manuscripts
Durham Cathedral
Lichfield Cathedral

Young Archaeologists Club
If you are interested in finding out more
about archaeology, you might like to join
the Young Archaeologists Club, United
House, Piccadilly, York YO1 1PQ.

Riddle's solution
The answer is a book. This riddle describes how a
dead animal's skin is prepared for writing on with a
quill pen.

Glossary

Ale   An old name for beer.

Archaeologist   A man or woman who studies history from remains found in the earth or under the sea.

Beeswax   The substance made by bees to form their combs.

Cask   Another name for a barrel.

Cemetery   A place where dead people are buried.

Charred   Blackened and burnt by fire.

Diet   All the different sorts of food and liquid someone eats and drinks.

Dormitory   A room where many people sleep.

Embroider   To sew patterns or pictures on to a piece of cloth.

Export   To send goods abroad to be sold.

Garment   An item of clothing.

Granary   A storehouse for wheat and other grains.

Hearth   The part of a floor on which a fire is made.

Kiln   An oven for hardening clay into pottery.

Linen   Cloth made from a plant called flax.

Loom   A machine for weaving cloth.

Mace   A long, heavy rod, often covered with decorations, used in ceremonies.

Mead   An alcoholic drink.

Missionary   Someone who goes to another country to spread his or her religion.

Pagan   A person who worships many gods.

Pedlar   A man or woman who travels around selling goods.

Taut   Stretched tightly.

Tunic   A long, short-sleeved jacket.

Yarn   Thread.

Books to read

Cork, B. & Reid, S. *The Young Scientist Book of Archaeology* (Usborne, 1984)

Jackson, R. *Dark Age Britain: What to See and Where* (Patrick Stephens, 1984)

Jones, D. *Your Book of Anglo-Saxon England* (Faber, 1976)

Kerr, N. & M. *A Guide to Anglo-Saxon Sites* (Granada, 1982)

Laing, L. & J. *The Young Archaeologist's Handbook* (Severn House, 1977)

Laing, L. & J. *Anglo-Saxon England* (Granada, 1982)

Page, R. *Life in Anglo-Saxon England* (Batsford, 1972)

Purves, A. *Growing up in a Saxon Village* (Wayland, 1978)

Ralph Lewis, B. *Growing up in the Dark Ages* (Batsford, 1980)

Triggs, T. *The Saxons* (Macdonald Educational, 1979)

Triggs, T. *The Saxons* (Oliver & Boyd, 1982)

Index

animals 9, 10, 12, 13, 14, 20, 29

Bede 5, 21, 25
Beowulf 18
bones 9, 13, 27
books 5, 21, 23

children 7, 19, 23
clothing 14, 15, 16, 17

death 9, 17, 18, 20, 24-5, 27
drink 12, 13, 18, 27

family life 6, 18-19, 27
farming 6, 12, 20
food 12-13, 23, 27

games 19
girdle hangers 27
graves 19, 24-5, 27

halls 6, 7, 18
helmets 25, 28
homes 6, 8-9, 15

illness 27

jewellery 17, 20, 24, 27

kilns 10-11
kings 12, 17, 21, 24-5, 29

looms 14-15

lyre 18

monasteries 5, 21, 22-3
money 24, 25
monks 5, 21, 23
music 18

Offa's Dyke 29

place names 5, 10, 12, 13, 19, 20
poor people 17, 26, 27
pottery 7, 8, 10-11, 13, 14

Redwald, King 21, 25, 28
religion 20-21, 23, 24, 29
rich people 16, 17
riddles 18-19
runes 20, 21

schools 23
slaves 27
spinning 14
sports 19
stories 18
Sutton Hoo 17, 24-5, 28

towns 17, 29

villages 6, 8-9, 10, 13

war 25, 27, 28-9
weaving 14-15, 17
West Stow 6, 8-9, 12